AF597345

Jesus Teaches Me CARING

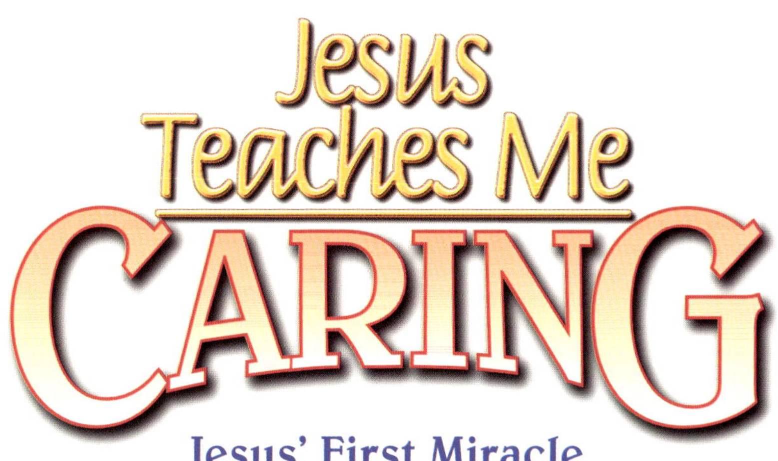

Jesus Teaches Me CARING

Jesus' First Miracle
Zacchaeus
Jesus Calms the Storm

An Inspirational Press Book for Children

Previously published as three separate volumes:

JESUS' FIRST MIRACLE

ZACCHAEUS

JESUS CALMS THE STORM

First Inspirational Press edition published in 1999.

Inspirational Press
A division of BBS Publishing Corporation
386 Park Avenue South
New York, NY 10016

Inspirational Press is a registered trademark of BBS Publishing Corporation.

Published by arrangement with Concordia Publishing House,
3558 S. Jefferson Avenue, St. Louis, MO 63118-3968.

Library of Congress Catalog Card Number: 98-75453

ISBN: 0-88486-230-5

Printed in Mexico.

JESUS' FIRST MIRACLE

John 2:1–11 for Children

Written by Vivian Dede
Illustrated by Chris Wold Dyrud

The people had gathered.
What feasting! What fun!

A marriage in Cana
Had finally begun.

Many guests were invited,
And Jesus came, too.

Plus disciples and Mary,
It made quite a few!

The disciples and Jesus
Sat down in their places,
But some of the people
Had frowns on their faces.

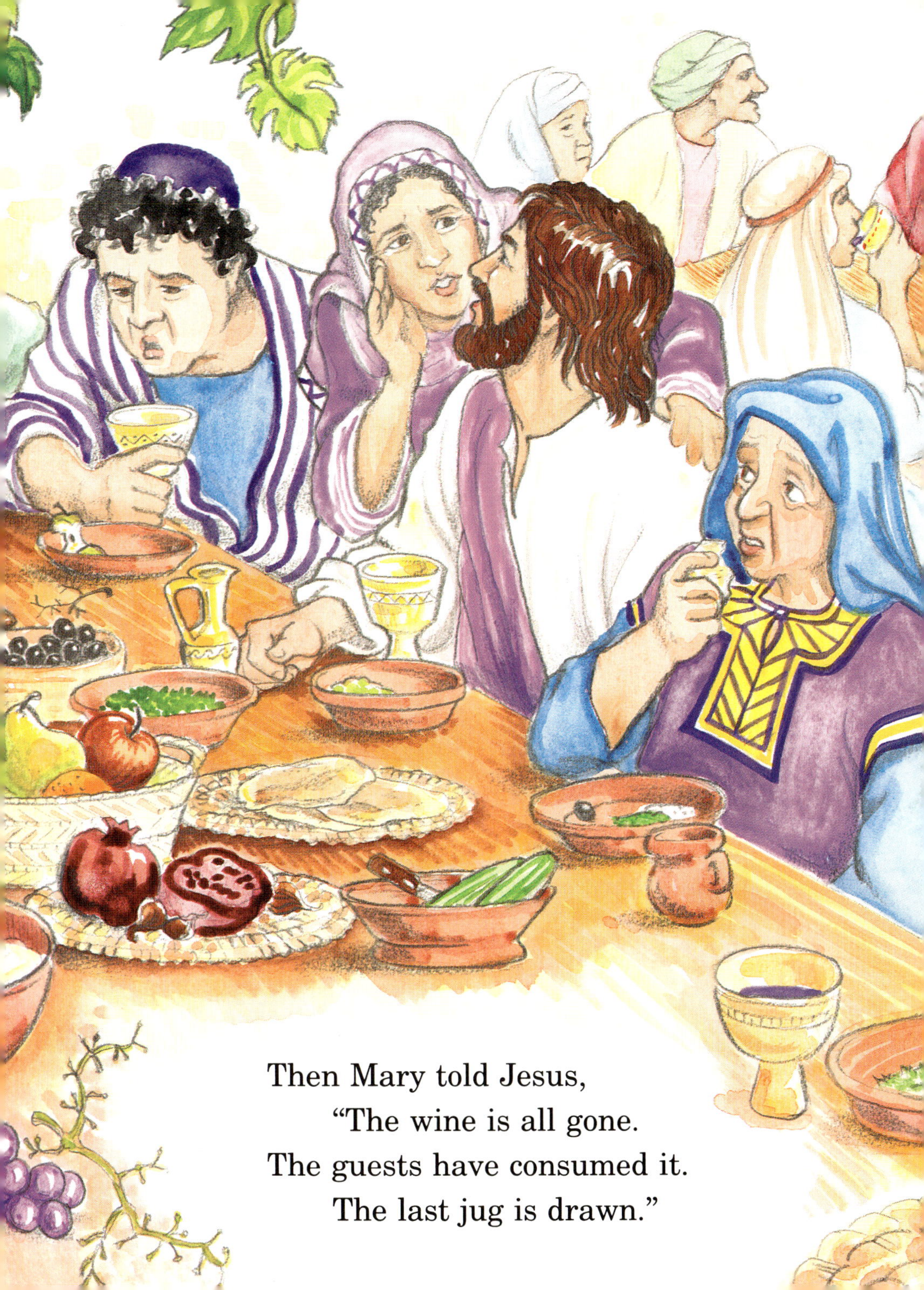

Then Mary told Jesus,
"The wine is all gone.
The guests have consumed it.
The last jug is drawn."

She trustfully waited,
Expecting her Son
Would know just exactly
What ought to be done.

“Dear Mother,” He answered,
“My time has not come.
When everything’s ready
My work will be done.”

Mary said to the servants,
"Do all that He asks."
They waited—were ready—
To learn their new tasks.

There sat in the courtyard
Six vessels of stone,
Used strictly for water
And water alone.

Each took many gallons
To fill to the rim,
But Jesus instructed,
"Fill each to the brim!"

With huffing and puffing
The servants obeyed,
Though secretly wondering
About efforts they made.

But as they were filling
The jars in a line,

All the water turned purple,
The color of wine!

Then Jesus commanded,
"Draw a cupful at least,
And take to the master
In charge of the feast."

The master was startled,
As tasting, wide-eyed,
He went to the bridegroom
And called him aside.

“Most people will furnish
Good wine at the first
When guests are most eager
To settle their thirst.

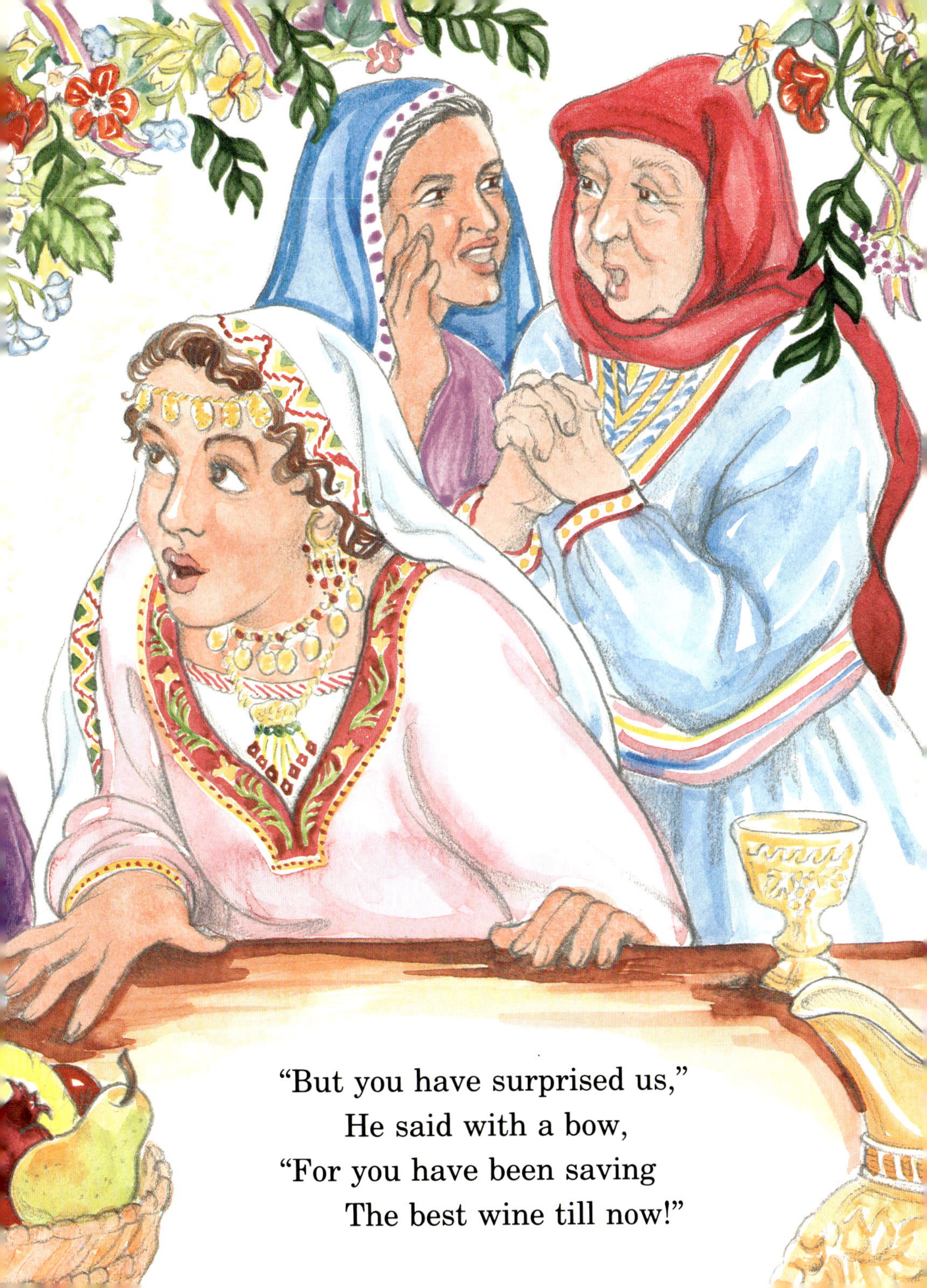

“But you have surprised us,”
He said with a bow,
“For you have been saving
The best wine till now!”

The disciples were awestruck
To see Jesus' power.

It made them believers
From that very hour.

They traveled with Jesus
And helped teach His Word.
And when people came to them
Here's what they heard:

"When something is needed,
Be it new life or wine,
Jesus solves every problem
In His own good time."

Dear Parents,

At the wedding at Cana Jesus performed His first miracle to reveal His glory as the Son of God. It is significant to point out to your children that Jesus' first miracle dealt with a relatively small matter—having something to drink at a party. In Biblical times there was not a large variety of beverages. Water was used for purifying, and people usually drank wine. Jesus blesses marriage by attending the wedding feast and then makes sure His host is not embarrassed by running out of wine.

Jesus watches over our lives, lovingly concerned with each detail, and gives us every good thing that we need. You might want to pray with your child and say thank You for all the "small things" God gives—favorite foods, special toys, happy occasions.

Notice that in this story Jesus changes the water to wine at His appropriate time. His reply to Mary that "My time has not yet come" (John 2:4) is not a brusque rejoinder, but simply a reminder that Jesus works according to His Father's ordained will. Similar expressions are used throughout the Gospel of John (John 7:6, 8, 30; 8:20). His time truly came when He gave His life on the cross and rose again to win eternal life for us.

From Jesus' first miracle on earth—changing water to wine—to His last act on earth—conquering sin and death—He shows loving concern for every great and small detail of our lives.

The Editor

Zacchaeus

Luke 18:35–19:9 for Children

Written by Loyal A. Kolbrek
Illustrated by James Needham

When Jesus came to Jericho,
Folks followed in a crowd.
Some of them were silent,
But some became quite loud.

They pleaded with the Savior
To heal them where they hurt.
Some so weak they couldn't stand
Were lying in the dirt.

Broken bodies, twisted limbs,
Eyes that could not see;
Now and then a feeble cry,
"Have mercy, Lord, on me."

The Savior loved them, every one,
And knew their faith was true.
He healed them with a gentle touch;
Their bodies, then, like new.

One man who gathered taxes
Was called a Publican.
The way he lived, he seemed to be
A very wealthy man.

The people all looked down on him,
For he was very short.
Zacchaeus had no friends in town;
They didn't like his sort.

Suddenly a shout went up:
"Jesus is coming near!"
And people ran to line the road,
Pushing to see and hear.

Zacchaeus saw the crowd and said,
"I wish that I were tall.
I'm much too small for this big crowd;
I cannot see at all."

Zacchaeus ran ahead and saw
A large and spacious tree.
He said, "I'll find a sturdy branch.
Then I can really see."

Zacchaeus climbed this sycamore
And watched the dusty trail.
He waited for the Lord to pass;
He'd see Him without fail.

The Lord looked up into the tree,
And people heard Him say,
"Zacchaeus, you come down here.
I'll visit you today!"

The crowd began to grumble,
"Should Jesus eat with him?
Zacchaeus lies and cheats us.
His life is full of sin.

"He steals a certain portion
Of taxes that we pay.
His purse is overflowing;
He gets richer every day!"

They didn't think the Savior
Should visit in his home.
They thought it would be better
To leave this crook alone.

Zacchaeus was quite flustered
At what the people said,
And as he walked with Jesus,
He simply bowed his head.

At home he turned to Jesus
And said, "I'm going to share
Half of my possessions
With those who need my care.

"And if I've cheated anyone,
I'll pay him four times more.
People here will see I've changed
From what I was before."

The Lord was pleased with what He heard
This tax collector say,
And said, “God’s free salvation
Has come to you today!”

Jesus came to seek the lost;
To set the sinner free.
He died and rose for each of us
And says, “Come, follow Me.”

DEAR PARENTS:

Children identify easily with Zacchaeus. They know firsthand what it feels like to be too short to see. And, sadly, they may have felt the sting of being teased or left out when older children are around.

Zacchaeus climbed a tree to get close to Jesus. Jesus used another tree—the tree of the cross—to win for us forgiveness, new life, and an invitation to eternal life with Him.

Zacchaeus made open confession of his sins and promised to give half his possessions to the poor and restore anything to which he was not entitled four times over—the Roman legal requirement for restitution for theft. Zacchaeus was a new man, a new creation in Christ. Celebrate your newness in Christ with your child.

THE EDITOR

Jesus Calms the Storm

Matthew 8:23–27
Mark 4:35–41
Luke 8:22–25
For Children
Written by Jean Thor Cook
Illustrated by Chris Wold Dyrud

Jesus was tired;
His hand covered a yawn.
The day had been busy,
From sunrise to sundown.

There'd been teaching and healing,
And stories to tell.
Many folks brought their sick,
And He made them well.

How could Jesus rest
With the crowd still there?
Why not sail ’cross the lake?
The disciples knew where.

The boat left the shore.
The crowd waved good-bye.
Jesus soon slept
Beneath the starry sky.

At first it was peaceful;
The waves splished and splashed.
But then a storm came up.
It came up so fast!

BANG! crashed the thunder.
It crackled, went *BOOM!*
Lightning zigzagged
And clouds hid the moon.

Jesus slept through it,
Cushion under His head—
Peaceful, relaxed,
As though in His bed.

The wind shrieked and moaned;
The boat gathered speed.
Why was Jesus sleeping?
His friends were in need!

“If this storm gets worse,”
They said with a cry,
“We’ll have to wake Jesus,
Before we all die!”

The boat rose and fell;
The sea waved in lumps.
The men were so frightened—
They had big goose bumps!

They grabbed the boat's oars
And rowed with strong might.
The little boat groaned
In the black of the night.

The water rose higher.
The friends had one wish—
Knees knocking, they hoped
Not to swim with the fish.

But the winds roared more fiercely.
Waves whooshed o'er the bow.
"We need to wake Jesus,
And do it right now!

"Don't you know we could perish?"
They questioned their Lord.
"Get up or we'll drown;
We'll be swept overboard!"

“Be quiet! Be still!”
Jesus spoke to the waves.
Quickly they calmed—
They had to obey.

Jesus asked His disciples,
"Why were you scared?
Have faith!" They'd forgotten—
Jesus always cared.

The disciples then wondered,
Who was this great man
Who brought them safe sailing,
Got them out of that jam?

He was awesome! Magnificent!
Full of power was He!
How did He take charge
Of those raging seas?

In time, they'd know Jesus
Was God's precious Son;
That His life would be given
To save everyone!

Dear Parents:

After reading this story, you might want to act it out by filling a pan with water. Sail a toy boat and blow on it with your child to create a storm. Then stop blowing and watch the storm end. Talk with your child about a time when you have been afraid. Help your child understand that we all feel afraid at times. Then read Psalm 56:3 together, "When I am afraid, I will trust in You."

Explain to your child that just as Jesus calmed the storm, He can calm our worries and fears and help us handle the problems that trouble us. He carried our greatest fear—fear of eternal death—to the cross and won our victory for us. Pray together with your child, thanking Jesus for His loving care.

The Editor